BLUE STONE

BLUE STONE & OTHER POEMS

Neva Herrington

STILL POINT PRESS · DALLAS

Copyright © 1986 by Neva Herrington

This book may not be reproduced, in whole or in part, in any form (beyond that copying permitted by Sections 107 and 108 of the 1976 U. S. Copyright Law and except by reviewers for the public press), without written permission from the publishers.

Library of Congress Cataloging-in-Publication Data
Herrington, Neva, 1926–
   Blue stone and other poems.

   I. Title.
PS3558.E7555B5 1985   811′.54   85-17269
ISBN 0-933841-02-7

For my children

CONTENTS

I   ORIGINAL

The Prince	3
If You Were a Character in Chekhov	4
A Sister's Wedding Party	5
According to Aristotle	6
Blue Stone	7
Six Widows at a Connecticut Beach Club	8
School of the Dance	9
Early American	10
Her Estate Now a State Park	11
Car	12
Ice Cream Truck	13
Original	14

II   THE FATHER MAKER

Poem for the Drinker	17
Disappearances	20
Rat Poem	21
Daughter in Texas	22
At San José Mission	24
Blind Broom Man	25
The Father Maker	26
Summer of a Writer	28
On Stanhope Street	29
Sunday Afternoon at White Rock Lake	30
Dallas Intersection	31

III   EAST TO PARENTS

Breakdown with Starlings	35
October	36
Thanksgiving House	37
East to Parents	38
Ouija	42
Lilacs	43
Disappointments	44

IV   KINGDOMS

Parallel	47
Grandmother Singing	48
Garlic	49
The Man Who Died of Fright	50
Dinosaur	51
A Tulip Cart	52
Kingdoms	53
Newcomers	54
Arrivals	55
The Bakery Sonnet	56
The Street People Refuse the City Shelter	57
The Fear of Bridges	58
Pot Holes	59
An Elegy Rose	60
Heart	61
The Movies	62
The Lover Is the Place	63
The Dentist's Walnut Tree	65
Poland	66
Public Pool	67

ACKNOWLEDGEMENTS

"A Sister's Wedding Party" appeared in *Commonweal*. "Car," "Rat Poem," "Blue Stone," "Disappearances," "According to Aristotle," "Kingdoms," and "The Bakery Sonnet" appeared in *Southwest Review*. "If You Were a Character in Chekhov" (under the title "Michael's Poem"), "Daughter in Texas," and "Grandmother Singing" appeared in *Inlet*. "Poem for the Drinker, I *Christmas*" (under the title "The Drinker's Christmas") and "Lilacs" appeared in *Ascent*. "Original" appeared in the *Southern Review*. "The Father Maker" appeared in *Wind Literary Journal*. Acknowledgement is also made to the Yaddo Corporation for a period of residence in 1976 during which some of these poems were written.

I
ORIGINAL

THE PRINCE

Meeting him first in a book, I saw him
For years in watercolor with blue cape
And stockinged legs. For him the woods unsnarled,
The house began to beat.

For years he ran parallel to his meaning
Like allegory in his pastel wood,
Fighting those last minute dinosaurs
To death in picture blood.

Years eat like dragons. The prince is turning
The pages. Each spring in the numbering grass,
Dandelions fatten like descendants,
The woods move toward a place.

IF YOU WERE A CHARACTER IN CHEKHOV

For MICHAEL

If you were a character in Chekhov,
You would be the one to say, "I will tear
Love out of my heart by the roots." As if

Anyone can. What can I do for you?
Drink, take pills, marry the wrong one, at some
Unpracticed moment you will know the lines

That are yourself. There's also the girl
Who in the last act will say it's good luck
To love even the one turning away.

Knowing love isn't a root or a part
But the light locating you in the dark
Performance. Love is out of your hands.

A SISTER'S WEDDING PARTY

For A. J. B.

Having known most of them before and since,
I search this time-brown photograph for signs:
Some warning missed. A post factum eye
Turning up history, not prophecy, makes
A lasting mystery not of what but why.
No answer in those nineteen smiling faces
Why some had secret, others bold disgraces.

Why the frogman turned homosexual and died
White-haired at thirty-eight or the kneeling man
With the flower girl is alcoholic or
The pilot crashed his plane, why some have lost
Only looks and tempers. One seems no more
Than another here lucky, bidden, exempt
By invitation from what could break or tempt

To death. Since I am there, I ought to have
The answer for myself at least. Do I
Know what I was that long ago? Afraid,
No doubt, I'd spoil the mother's show, there
Because the second born, the honor maid,
Hoping against all law of bone and blood
To come out more beautiful than I could.

ACCORDING TO ARISTOTLE

Driving home from Shakespeare, the children said
the Juliet was old: You have to look
that part. Meanwhile April was going on.
Serious and of a certain magnitude,
trees here and there were turning red.

Older than Juliet I didn't tell them
love will turn to blood and only the play
holds still, love fixed in its surprise.
Meanwhile the lovers go to bed,
children in red running woods.

BLUE STONE

The worst tourist in Scotland takes
scenes as they come, treads down castles,
hears monuments explained from a bus,
rides through a town of empty streets

always deserted, the driver says,
like towns in American Westerns,
on foot to a famous height sinks
in burrs and mud, creeps damp stones

to a dungeon latrine, marches on jewels,
rooms of prayers and blood, leaves
the film in the camera so long
only a miracle could keep it true,

remembers finally the blue stone
on the northern beach, flat as a table,
true to its one color, some
solitary plot of its own.

SIX WIDOWS AT A CONNECTICUT BEACH CLUB

Six widows at a porch table
in garden-colored knit shirts
bare tanned, withered arms and throats.
One wears a straw hat, ribbon trimmed.
Under the table is a basket of bottles:
scotch, bourbon, gin, white wine, dubonnet,
gem colors poured in noon sunlight.

Drinking, they watch an elderly pair,
wraiths in slacks and jackets, enter
from the clubhouse. Her iron gray hair
is chopped square like the hair of the condemned
to the guillotine in old films.
She carries the basket. His face
is ashen. His white hands hang down.

A space goes with them like a spotlight
haltingly into the June glare.
The widow in the hat says: "I heard
they drank all winter!"
                        A seagull
flies to the porch railing too near
the widows' table, flares winter
colors fresh from the summer sea.

SCHOOL OF THE DANCE

A skeleton rises, mine, undoes a backbone
As if it were a ribbon, shoulders down,
Swings the arms around then back the other way.
A late beginner, I'm moving circumstances
Not bones and muscles. History dances
Every time. Stretching and bending, I pray

For what's already done, prophesy
The present, and that's control, don't try
For the leap that holds in air or even pretend
I could break a body like spirit, make
It a new thing as if it were no thing, a fake,
Risking in this routine my only end.

EARLY AMERICAN

This early American bed is no
roped off museum relic, no idle,
rare ornament for a poet to make
splendors of; the four pencil posts and foot
high headboard in solid maple are simple
enough for the earliest American believing
design held up as the woods backed off.

Children, like early Americans, sleep
afraid of the dark of the woods next door.
Only a child asleep, rolling over
the side of an early American bed
and under, could wake up and touch the dark turned
solid overhead and believe for a minute
the sky could come down to the palm of a hand.

HER ESTATE NOW A STATE PARK

Touring a museum house in spring
when the branches of the big trees
become a red network in the sky,
we linger at tiled fireplaces,
blank with cold
in the deliberate emptiness
of her aging mansion's change of life.

Only the window views are personal,
still hold in place her sea and park.
We can't renew these vacant rooms
with our strange, sporadic blood
and the house done,
walk like pets let out past boxwood
cut to the initials of her name.

In her Chinese garden, the beds
between the pebble paths are tilled
and sown now to follow her plan
of summer flowers. Her stone buddahs
withhold like stone.
Paying thieves, we take our time
as gardens change to gardens.

CAR

Where the sand is cold an inch down
We built the car, dug hard in blue
Grey sand for floors, beat sliding walls
To seats and dashboard, stuck shells
For lights and worked a driftwood wheel:
Our car, our way of riding out
The adult beach, their made-up world
Where ropes laid down the shore and sharp
Umbrellas trimmed the sun. We drove
Toward water all afternoon alive.

Thirty years from that car, we watch
The tide move another beach, shells,
Driftwood washing down the shore
Now of a sea where years have spilled
Wrong cargoes, black, ranging oils
Under those deep blue patchwork calms,
And the ships taking shape miles out,
Ask if there is beyond the dark
Down life that drinks and holds all poisons
Some last reform of all our treasons.

ICE CREAM TRUCK

No bicycle bell
rang down those hills
like the ice cream truck
one summer,
clearing the streets
of every afternoon.

As if an ancient king
whose touch could heal
were making a progress
through his kingdom,
slowly,
like a proclamation,

the bell rang
neighborhoods away,
drawing the distance out
along the old route.

ORIGINAL

Those woods are a space now,
a fixed outline, a painting
you spoil every day,

trying to make the seasons fit
exactly as if the blackbirds
weren't racing in pairs

on either side of a line,
and the white moths of July
filling the small jar of the air

weren't the one thing you carried
alone into all that snow saying:
Woods are for lovers,

the sun singling you out
among stems poised in their sap,
walking to a welcome

where no bird sings for an answer
as if a song had to touch a song
in perfect time.

II
THE FATHER MAKER

POEM FOR THE DRINKER

I
Christmas

Six stories high in an old hotel, you see
The river you, a hero, rode one war.
You could dive to the deepest safety then.
Death was a place that happened only once.

Now days go deep. You ride them in this room,
Captain of four walls you still can pay for.
You take yourself down like a careful ship
Past the depth charge of every lived-out year.

High as your window, the steeple clock
Moves in the dark. Every hour hits.
Downstairs the streetlights go on like harbors,
The gold foil angels far away and small.

II
The Eagle's Nest

Saying goodbye at the airport,
You looked ahead through dark glasses,
Held the arms of the waiting-room chair
As we waved to make you see us.

Those three years you lived in a room
You named the eagle's nest, you said
You needed more time. Your landlord
Found you one night staring and cold.

We had nothing to do but see
When we examined in that room
The soiled dark arms of your one chair
Where you had gripped three years.

III
Fort Sam Houston

A mourner, your former wife,
At the December noon burial
In the south Texas fort,
I heard you were no one's:

Coffin wheels on metal runners
Under a plastic canopy,
Taps for a Captain lost
Long after the war,

A back and forth bulldozer
Leading a column of graves
Beyond the grass on the buried
And the young mimosas' shade.

DISAPPEARANCES

No one saw the cattle killed in Texas
and their genitals stolen or the woods
in Tennessee take down a house. One old
lady you know of had a doctor stop
the music in her head. Innocent concerts
of Mozart stuck like malice in her ears.

Some people can make you disappear, an act
of the will they think and proud of it.
You yourself don't know when you'll turn up
in his head with all the scenery of real
romance, his mother dead, and you fair
as a resident tune after a long absence.

RAT POEM

On a hot night in mid-November,
I heard them, blood serious,
making arrangements over my head.
I lay in the dark listening
to my place in a house.

I'd always trusted divisions,
believing the dead were safe.
Those rats were so sure of my house,
establishing themselves in structure
as if it were proof.

DAUGHTER IN TEXAS

From one fall to another south
Two thousand miles was the move
We had to make. That year the trees
Were strangers: live oak, cottonwood,
Mimosa, red bud, that one we
Couldn't understand, mock orange
With its hard, green fruit, all surface
And fake meat like our change.

For years like an expert mime you
Placed New England a locked house
Around you. At sixteen, three years
Away, you made a subject of one
Mock orange from the tree in our yard,
Drew every knotted line in pale
Pencil as if to touch too hard
Might break you. That bumpy rind looked frail

As you, attentive to its own
Design. The next fall you went south
To college. Your drawings darkened,
More accurate than you could bear.
Your friends on mescaline with lovers,
The year you chose to lose a child,
Went down like windfall fruit. You lived
Without touching anywhere.

Still making up your mind to what
You are, you say you've spoiled yourself
With too much time with too much place.
For years I saw our mock orange
Huddle its fallen fruit inward
As if still bearing those broken rinds.
I bless your children never born,
The green fruit shaping our hands.

AT SAN JOSÉ MISSION

For R. B. H. (1920–1974)

No tourist, you took the centuries
personally. Those facts had stayed
together: crude huts for soldiers,
grass in the monastery garden,
the monks' house only stone doorways.
There was so much light everywhere
everything seemed proved and over.

The window carved in stone for love
of a woman was another matter.
That small, particular light
asked nothing. Faithful praise
for centuries was no proof at all
the most solid dark might yield
to love and hold it as it was.

BLIND BROOM MAN

The blind broom man comes back,
asking the number of my house.
But you've been here before! The brooms
tremble; he shields them with his stick.
Are you sure you wouldn't like something more?
I hear his stick placing the darkness
as he goes down the walk. Why should I fear
what I pity? I see the hardness
of light, the colors shutting the door.

THE FATHER MAKER

Marked with pipes, circled by one neighbor,
your fifteen acres are no farm.
The gate is yours, the right of way
to the line of oaks the deed says
begins your land. Eight months after
you died alone, your only son
and I entered your only kingdom.

In the Texas August, six-inch grass
pricked and buzzed. We watched the herd
a farmer grazes there by contract,
dug up a stiff-rooted bush to plant
on a bank of the water hole you stocked.
That muddy tank can't keep fish,
the farmer says, is too narrow to clear.

Nevertheless, we go back to sink
fresh branches to make green life.
In fall and winter, not much changed.
The frizzled trees shed copper leaves,
looked like old men not grown enough.
The cows were friendlier, had calves
and lost their teeth and looks by spring.

If they're lucky, people don't change.
They clear. This deed is the word
you couldn't speak. Around us are scenes
you didn't describe: the radiant tractor
stopped in sunset, the field where horses
touch in sleep. Your land. Now your son's.
Here seasons are words in the earth.

SUMMER OF A WRITER

The summer I sat at a window and typed,
A crow lived in the trees beyond the creek.
Floppy winged, big as a vulture, he flew
Every now and then across what I saw.
I kept looking for another, a mate,
Kept listening for an answer to the caw
I would hear from time to time, but none came.
It seemed like me he lived a lonely rite.

Eventually I didn't like the crow.
That self-sufficiency I thought was his
Frightened me more than the old saying one
Crow means bad luck. He was an omen
Over and over, a blackness writing
Hints concerning the bad luck of one woman
Searching the woods of one crow for luck,
For wings of another, that friend: the grand alighting.

None came. At last I watched his grove of trees
As if I lived in them myself, as if
They were myself, locality that's friend.
I am not a graveyard where no one speaks
Except the visitors. I am the dead
Saying what they might have said, talk that breaks
Like wings, the blackest wings, through leaves toward light.
I heard the crow. Good luck to you, I said.

ON STANHOPE STREET

The house on Stanhope Street didn't fail us.
A meadow ran at our fence. A night train
rode a block away, shaking our walls.
Its whistle rang like a final ritual.

We ran to reach the track before the light
could turn around the dark, as if to see
that humming halo start meant our good luck,
the meadow moving seasons at our back.

Night after night walking home
to the light of our house so stopped and still,
we welcomed the meadow like a neighbor
welcoming us all the way to our door.

SUNDAY AFTERNOON AT WHITE ROCK LAKE

Across the lake the harbor
was a bundle of ashen sticks.
The trees were still as carvings.
Your father hid in the car
with gin and the Mormon choir
while you and I went walking.

You wanted to sit in the rowboat,
bedded deep in reeds,
the floor an inch in water
but the seats dry enough.
You steered from a bow that swayed
toward its length of hemp rope.

You said we were sailing for joy.
I cleared my head for a poem.
The car on the hill was dark
when finally we got back,
your father asleep at the wheel
over the news and weather.

DALLAS INTERSECTION

For J. F.

A stranger riding by one night
stopped to die. The voice at the door
asking to let the sick man in
was angry. I telephoned for help,
looked finally after the siren
was louder than Haydn on the stereo,
saw him lighted like a celebration
down on my lawn, facing the sky,
the man in the ambulance in no hurry
writing while five policemen
walked around the light they'd made.
Why talk? A man dies where he is
In a dark yard, the silence he makes
could be a trick or a cry.

III
EAST TO PARENTS

BREAKDOWN WITH STARLINGS

That winter every afternoon
the starlings came for bread. They ate,
then flew away in one body.

I watched from a bedroom window
in a small, rented house. That winter
I didn't throw bread to birds.

No cure can be single and sure
as starlings flying. Every day
that winter my yard was light as bread.

OCTOBER

For N. P. J.

Take one last look at a New England scene,
said Mother, believing still in landscapes.
I looked and saw a pale green, empty hill.

My father said I wouldn't know the place
in a year. He would fill that hill with trees,
a hill of Christmas trees to cut and sell.

When I turned at the road, I said to myself:
If I see them, I'll come back. Not yet bare,
a red maple hid them. I saw the hill.

THANKSGIVING HOUSE

That sister's was the house we thought of last
for Thanksgiving dinner after her husband
left. He always cooked the turkey and trimmings
and told her what pies to bake for in-laws
who shook his ornament house for their pleasure.

The spring I was her guest overnight, North
after years Southwest, I didn't notice
her sleeping alone in the living room
or the dwarf orange tree in the hall she said
had a breakdown from five children fighting.

And she had no time for the late April
snowfall I rushed outside to see
melt in warm winds, snow dissolving in earth
her husband had turned over for summer,
swirling to nothing in the grey bright air.

EAST TO PARENTS

I

Train riding east to parents,
I play I'm coming back.
I'm trying to learn the role,
Nothing I could forget:
Some art or trick I lack.

The station where no one meets me
Signals facts like a dream.
The river hasn't run out.
The town's in place. Things are
Exactly what they seem.

And I'm their two-eyed daughter,
Riding in a taxi alone
To a house I won't recognize
Over a road I don't know,
Directed by telephone.

It's their last house, they say.
They've looked for their address
Too long. Something I said
In another house has made
Them angry. We don't kiss.

Telling the truth that once
Was for no one's sake.
The golden calf is gone.
There's no time for dancing
Though all the laws break.

II

Every morning I wake up in this bed
I know who I am.
I unroll like a story on a scroll,
Someone hard to love, too near to blame.

Spoiler of gardens, Marvell's, and all the way back
To the first one,
Rib, afterthought, mischief maker, greedy,
In my parents' house, I know what God has done

And wait, scared and bold as a child, braving
This too long reprimand.
Inheritor of my own heart, I ask
For their blessing, hold out my hairless hand.

III

Three clocks strike every hour all night long
and two the half hour; two sing songs and one
simply chimes. Their pendulum hearts are strong
to say mere things take care, the hours run.

I hear their dry tunes again in my child-
hood bed not as truth but noise; the same chimes
that forced love, wedding, births tell me I'm old,
and clocks keep me awake telling their times.

I told my father one sleepless night can't hurt.
Without a word he reached and stopped each heart.

IV

The sun is coming up like a toy,
brightest ball in the nursery corner.
In the harbor the boats are put away.
The train track winds and shines.
The only one awake in the house,
I watch this sun's small neighborhood
aging to a fresh start.

One of a kind in the family ark
must be quiet as the glass-eyed animals
the children take to bed at night,
magic for the dark, for the dove
back again with no ground for the house.
Make room. The pairs are working in blood.
The sun is crossing its own light.

OUIJA

No tree like that one blooms anywhere else
I know of. Every other year it showered
white petals on the brick walk to our door.
The suitors came with flowers in their hair
like blessings, foreseen by the one, round eye
of the ouija board, family friend, ogling
our destinies over our crowding knees.
Most of the time that pointer moved to please.

Proving, glib oracle, that what counts
are questions. That eye circled for mates
like targets, reported the day, the month, the year
the war would end. Respectable spook, how
could we doubt your combinations? Your talk
was clearer than a tree, blessing or not.
Out of your sharp cornered world, your yes and no,
the answers spelled. Only the names came true.

LILACS

For J. R. J. (1899–1977)

On my parents' lawn, the lilac trees are single,
small, and frail in beds of yellow stones.
My father tends them this cold morning, says
he loves spring for lilacs. I ask him
if he remembers lilac trees so close
they made a house for children. He nods,
glad of this image he doesn't fail.

In his seventy-sixth year, my father
thinks himself into position around
each tree. The blood that runs him hardens.
He stops to plan the rising of his hand,
watches its halting route, then waits to walk
till the ground is sure of him. In one morning
I count more than a dozen starts in terror.

At noon, his voice gone with the morning's work,
he picks a basket of lilacs. Between us
on the table, they are solid as walls
of a tree house waving in light in days
when a garden could grow from anyone's hand,
and the voices calling from windows: Time
to come home, children, time, were forever.

DISAPPOINTMENTS

In her old age, front teeth darkened,
Two missing, hand trembling for Scotch
In a crystal glass, she who found fault

With every house couldn't account
For the memory of a daughter
Opposite her at the table

(A Jacobean work of art)
Set with a nail file and mirror
And papers she wouldn't sign

Any longer as now and then
She brought the mirror to her face
To touch a neck curl or her cheek

While the daughter saw houses ago
A cherry tree in the garden
Of a just bought house, her mother

Out for once in the June sunlight,
At ease among strangers' plantings,
Her small hand pointing to cherries

Without dislike for her daughter
On a ladder filling a bowl
With only the fruit having no blemish.

IV
KINGDOMS

PARALLEL

For M. R.

Level with roofs on a fenced porch,
I have the sky to myself tonight.
My neighbor's charcoal broiling fire
sends up a small and seasoned smoke
to my six-by-nine shelf.

Over my head are more shelves
than the smoke can touch. In the east
rising girders hold the sunset
like a ladder. A bird calls in English:
Kill, kill, kill to the mild air.

Stranger below, in such neighborhoods
of place only, our loneliness holds on
like love or any unfinished thing.
Space is the hold around us
in a high-rise night.

GRANDMOTHER SINGING

The backstairs were a box of light
the morning I heard you sing
in our house, Grandmother, ready
for the Met at twenty-two, caught
by a rich old man of your own choosing.
No bird, you swallowed your voice, medicine
that made you sicker. That loud, bad
digestion embarrassed the whole
family who didn't know music.
Nobody knows why you left the concert
at "Goodbye, my Beloved," weeping,
why I heard you in that walled,
narrow staircase with the window
at one end as if one time were all
in a shaft of a thousand motes blazing.

GARLIC

Sure of its medicinal punch,
I'm not scared off by the news story
of the boy who choked in his sleep
and died with garlic in his throat
to ward off vampires.

The ceramic garlic house,
a temple with holes for breathing,
holds a nugget that scours lungs,
loosens the clog in the bloodstream,
terrorizes worms.

Entering my house after a while
elsewhere, the odor of garlic
from a remnant lodged in the wide
throat of the disposal sometimes
embarrasses me

with the truth I've taken garlic
as many have taken lovers
for worse not better. This pungent bud,
purple-veined and green-hearted, hustles
my rank solitude.

THE MAN WHO DIED OF FRIGHT

On the night before his operation
in a room to himself, the man waits
who told you he was afraid.
His heart blunders on a graph,
knocks and misses in the cold ear
of the stethoscope, will heal only
in violence, a new blood route,

is the heart of a man who believes
he goes, no king, to his last dragon
among clamps and needles and basins
shining and the masked agents who do
not run away and their chief, scholar
of knives, who hasn't a chance with him,
who, sleeping with open hands, will die,

who imagines himself now
before the last drug of the night,
the washings, the obedient sleep,
sprung from his cotton shoes, his gown
strung at the neck, and this empty room
with no footprint, no blood to tell
where he might have run.

DINOSAUR

Game of bones, styrofoam
Tyrannosaurus Rex,
one tenth your living size
in an attic with outgrown toys:
trucks, soldier dolls, a train,
the book with the picture of you
tearing the flesh of a sauropod
in a sunset swamp with tropical trees,
your vacancies rebuild.
Here plastic holds you light
as paper, local as bones
holding their own.

A TULIP CART

Walking outside after teaching
Sophocles' death of Oedipus
—that extraordinary vanishing!—
to my eight o'clock class who rise
always immediately at the bell,

I saw roll up the ramp a cart
of tulips from the greenhouse lab,
all reds and yellows in pots crammed
to its sides, wheels turning fast
following so closely the death of Oedipus.

KINGDOMS

Up after surgery,
heads thrust forward,
hands on abdomens,
stitched tight as new pillows,
the women in GYN
walk to the window

at the end of the hall,
for a moment pay
absolute attention
to a whitewashed wall,
a parking lot,
three scraggy trees

wired upright
in the summer heat,
slowly turn back,
their IVs lurching
after them, on foot
in their hospital raiment.

NEWCOMERS

The bread factory's welcome
is the smell of bread in the street.
The house next door we named
the house of the crazy birds.

The owner we've yet to meet
hung a birdhouse in every tree.
The shadows go back and forth
over the same ground.

ARRIVALS

At eight every summer morning
I shut the window unit off,
cold as the cold machine stopped
in a hot garden, sealed at the sill.

The motor was loud as an engine
and tamer than passengers we slept
while the light moved into our room
like a stranger taking notes.

Some mornings I thought I could hear
moments after I'd turned the switch,
every cold object tick, morning
itself stalled in the window frame.

THE BAKERY SONNET

Sunday afternoons when Mr. Goldman
visits the bakery, there's always a crowd.
Everyone takes a number, mills among
the exhibits: round, tan loaves piled like stones,
triangle pastries gaudy as tropical fish,
yellow cakes, halved to show the brown marble.
At his turn, he doesn't deliberate,
points here, there, today (sighing) permits
another, the special, a three-fruit ring,
turns to the ones still waiting, says to them:
Have you noticed everyone here is fat?
A few laugh. Solemn now, he bears the boxed
weight, the scarlet cherry, the gold apricot
to kindle the house where his thin wife waits.

THE STREET PEOPLE REFUSE THE CITY SHELTER

Passing up supper, shower, bed,
they enter the winter night, small
to them now as a place worn thin
at the threshold, bottles held close,
their own names like secret messages
in the wrong hands.

                        The oil drum fire
lights up the heart, the head, the life
lines of cupped hands into itself.
There's light enough. The stars are clear
in this cold, are personal as sleep.

THE FEAR OF BRIDGES

Following a red pickup truck
downhill on the Cooper River Bridge,
I saw a man crouched on its hood
waving, his other hand on the wheel,
steering the truck close to the rail,
then over a bank at the end.
Falling under his wheels, he died.

Brakes fail anywhere. That terror
has nothing to do with the fear
over and over between shores.
A bridge that high and narrow lasts
as long as your hands hold on and steer,
only in a rearview mirror,
if you think to look, disappears.

POT HOLES

They keep records of them
like criminals or earthquakes.

Today the road crew
is patching this street,

rolling down stones and pitch,
crowding the pigeons

to the sidewalks, the roofs,
to my window ledge

where they establish their colors
this noon for one witness.

AN ELEGY ROSE

They say Queen Elizabeth feared roses,
and I'm no gardener though I'm planting a rose,
Father, on your birthday. I've dug through roots
tough as knotted twine.

                    Here April is cold
under a pale sun, the soil is stony,
and there's a wind through these leafless stumps, raw
from the greenhouse, the root in a cardboard box
which must go into the ground with the rose.

There are courtesies in the wildest field
unheard of in a formal garden. Goldenrod,
Queen Anne's lace, the yellow daisy die
without accusation whereas one spot
on a rose leaf condemns a gardener who
remembers your perfect roses.

                          Father, for you
I lower this rose, another transient,
in a box that melts as the root moves out.

HEART

For Joseph Shuman

Remember how it boomed in the walls
of the Hemisfair heart exhibit,
the miles of blood on the screen?
In the hospital emergency room,
the tape bunched and coiled at the machine
like news from the stock exchange.

Now you are fenced in a high bed,
tilted at thirty degrees, hooked up
to the cardiac unit screen, a live
performance that could go haywire.
All night you are a celebrity.
Even your dreams make waves.

The small black box slaps your back
as you turn over; the plugs suck
at your skin. You won't die alone.
At that Hemisfair in Texas,
South American Indian acrobats
circled high in the air with torches.

That was the year American nuns
shortened their skirts and let out
their faces. Three on our bench watched,
heads thrown far back, those fires go
around a pole higher than anywhere
in San Antonio for the first time.

THE MOVIES

For you at twelve love had the taste
of chocolate softening in foil in your lap.
Hitler moved jerkily on the screen.
That early you accepted the role
of spectator, swallowing the war
with Hershey bars: the black oceans,
the white explosions performed in static,
Fred Astaire dancing like bullets.

Middle-aged, at a twin drive-in, alone
in the front seat of your compact car
rocking with children stretched on the hood,
you watch the Germans losing again
in technicolor on the east screen.
Over your west shoulder, R-rated love
lights a twin meadow of huddled metal.
Ahead a man blows up in his own field.

Your car is dark as a soldier's tent
under a wartime sky. The groans
of actors adjust to your ear.
Tonight east and west go out as one.
Calm, you join the slow procession
of cars let loose from their metal poles
as if only the stories end,
the children already asleep.

THE LOVER IS THE PLACE

For MAUREEN MCCABE

As they used to a dozen years
ago, the cars drive very fast
by Maureen's house this May, season
in Connecticut for dogwood.
Today in her house, I marvel
at the dogwood's efficient change
from white flowers to blood red leaves
flying in an October wind.

Jon, who lived here seven years, left
his doves. Their cries from a back room
cage shudder among the wicker chairs,
glass treasure case, papier-maché
monsters threaded in midair, glares
of assorted masks, ornaments
alive and secretive, fortune
telling in the one P.M. rain light.

In the room below, Maureen makes
her montages from beads, feathers,
pages of rare books, postcards, shells
she found on the Northwest Irish
seacoast, naming them Crough Patricks
after the holy mountain she
didn't climb. Over such objects
her thin white arms hover hours,

sewing, glueing, tacking, tracing
letters and words so the magic
will hold in the clear plastic box.
Across the hall, Jon's abandoned
studio holds only clutter.
Above that room the dove lays eggs
she refuses to sit on. Old
and neurotic, she can't stand birth.

One summer an egg hatched from heat
alone in a record heat wave.
I saw a pink, yellow-veined claw
stretch out from under the mother
who once the child was there made room.
Growing, it showed a weakness, legs
too frail to launch a flight. Maureen
herself helped it into the air,

dove therapy for months before
the exit trip to the vet's. Near
the cage Maureen keeps the small white
eggs, years of them, in a deep bowl,
fragile tombs in a neighborhood
of the parents' randy racket,
at midday a still life flying
with all the seasons of dogwood.

THE DENTIST'S WALNUT TREE

For F. M.

Early for his first job of the day
—my five day dying right front tooth—
I study the sun-kindled leaves,
yellowing and loose in late October,
of an ancient, half-dead walnut
the narrow, open window frames.

I'm bibbed and drugged and left alone.
From all directions sparrows fly
to the tree's living lower half.
They bounce on thin branches, shake free
more leaves, exit in one rising
over the desolate top limbs.

The dentist comes back. I tell him
I like his tree. He says the tree
needs doctoring but isn't his.
At the joints of his drill's long arm
the discs are spinning. A hook drains
saliva into a whirling bowl.

My mouth is loud as a building site.
I breathe my dust, my tooth calcined
into my elements. The root
sealed, the dentist offers mouthwash.
Behind him, the ailing walnut
looks ready for the next patient.

POLAND

For B. G.

After her mother's ten-year silence
was diagnosed as hopeless and her
father refused to give her mother
to the hospital to keep, she found
the Polish woman's shop, a gallery
of sculptures, paintings, tapestries, prints,
and crafts from Poland.

Her walls made room for the Polish art
she could buy with funds her father sent
(saved those years he tended her mother):
the fisherman in sunset water
who recalls her father, the resort
forest church on Christmas eve lighted
for frozen strangers.

Long afternoons she watches Poland:
mauve reflections in a city street
(next to the church scene), the roses so
securely painted to their vases,
the horses' heads at the painting's rim
with lifesize expressions and their farm
as safe as Poland.

PUBLIC POOL

For B. W.

On my back, watching the sky change to night,
I swim between the children playing ball,
the boy and girl signalling love without
dividing anyone from anyone,
bumping no one in underwater light.

Beyond the chain link fence, houses let go
darkening boundaries to a dark that floats
bread fragrance from a bakery oven blocks
away while we in our guarded water,
vessels in bathing suits, swim laps in lanes.

A star comes out. The lovers divide
to swim, slip easily from each other here
where so many are flying neutral flags.
At the closing horn, I race for a ladder,
crossing all lines at emergency speed.

Neva Herrington was born in New London, Connecticut, and was educated at schools in Connecticut, South Carolina, and Texas. She has been a teaching fellow at Southern Methodist University, where she earned the M.A. degree in English. She has also taught at the Williams School in Connecticut and at Richland College in Texas. She is presently on the faculty of Northern Virginia Community College.

A resident at Yaddo in 1976, and at the Virginia Center for the Creative Arts in 1982 and 1984, Herrington was awarded *Southwest Review*'s first Stover poetry prize for her poem "Blue Stone." In addition to poetry, she has published critical articles and fiction. She is now living in Alexandria, Virginia.